O
OPRAH WINFREY

THE GIRL WHO WOULD GROW UP TO BE

Volume I

Words by A.D Largie

Pictures by Sabrina Pichardo

FIND ALL OUR OTHER BOOKS ON AMAZON
SEARCH FOR "keMeTToYS"

JOIN OUR MAILING LIST
AND GET FREE BOOKS

KEMET TOYS
KemetToys.com

WE LOVE 5-STAR REVIEWS
PLEASE LEAVE ONE

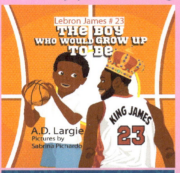

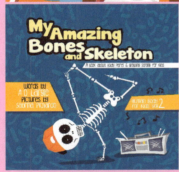
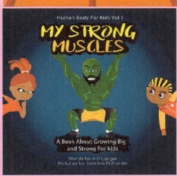
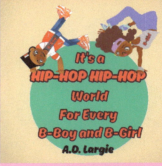

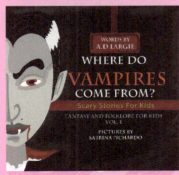

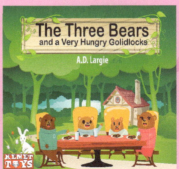

Once upon a time in a place called Mississippi a girl named **Orpah** was born in **Kosciusko City.**

Many people could not pronounce her name so they called her **Oprah** but she answered all the same.

When Oprah was a little girl she lived with her Grandma and they were **very poor.**

She would also get a spanking if she did not do her chores.

Oprah's grandma taught her to read when she was just **3 years old** because her grandma was very strict and **Oprah** did as she was told.

Oprah's grandma loved going to Church and would take little Oprah with her. Young Oprah was so good at reading the bible that they called her **the Little Preacher.**

Oprah **loved** her grandma very much and when she had to move away she felt very sad. For the next few years **her life got really bad.**

Life got better when Oprah started high school. Though she was still very poor **her talent for speaking** made her pretty cool.

Oprah became an honor student and was voted the **most popular girl** in school. She finally found her purpose and **had all the tools.**

When it came to speaking **Oprah had a firm grip** she competed in speech competitions and **won a full college scholarship**

Once Oprah **got a taste for winning she grabbed everyone's attention.**

She even won a **beauty pageant** and got hired as a **reporter at a radio station.**

Oprah became a news reporter at a very young age but it was Oprah's grandma who first knew **she had a talent for the stage.**

Oprah made history when she became the youngest and **first Black Woman to host a Nashville, Tennessee TV Show.**

But it was just the **beginning** for **Oprah's show** she became even **BIGGER** when she moved to **Chicago.**

While in **CHICAGO** Oprah took over a **TV show** that no body know about and turned it into **the most POPULAR** show **without** a doubt.

The television station renamed it **The Oprah Winfrey Show** and expanded it across the entire nation.

THE OPRAH
WINFREY SHOW
LIVE YOUR BEST LIFE

Oprah's show was a **big success** she invited the most famous **celebrities.** She was so bless.

Finally Oprah **became RICH.**
She wrote books, owned radio and TV
stations and produced
movies without
a glitch.

Oprah's opinion gained so much respect for Authors, Celebrities and Politicians. Businessmen, charities and major companies all wanted to have the **Oprah Effect.**

Of all her jobs **Oprah loves her work** as a humanitarian, she gave scholarships to children in America and built a school for girls in **South Africa.**

Oprah says she does not believe in failure and you shouldn't either. **Try your best and you will be an achiever**.

OPRAH WINFREY

A.D LARGIE

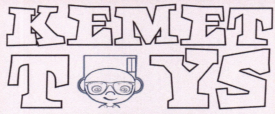

KemetToys.com

CPSIA information can be obtained
at www.ICGtesting.com
Printed in the USA
LVHW072344070319
609944LV00002B/8/P